· Q SERIES

Kes

a play by Barry Hines and Allan Stronach

Lance Hattatt and James Sale

Series editors: Lance Hattatt and James Sale

HODDER AND STOUGHTON

LONDON SYDNEY AUCKLAND TORONTO

Preface

Q Series is a series of English/Drama booklets for use with mixed-ability groups in the middle years of the secondary school. Standing independently of the text to which it relates, each booklet explores a well-known play through an informal but developing pattern of plot, character, theme, language and theatre.

Each section invites 'dipping-in'. Pupils will discover a wide range of lively and stimulating activities. These vary from discussion to writing, from recording to acting, and are designed to provide insight into a number of relevant and interesting topics.

Key to Logos

Drama work

Oral work for GCSE

Open study for GCSE

Writing for GCSE

British Library Cataloguing in Publication Data
Hines, Barry
Kes: a play. —— (Q Series).
1. Secondary schools. Activities: Drama – For schools
I. Title II. Stronach, Allan
III. Hattatt. Lance IV. Hines, Barry.
Kestrel for a knave V. Series
792'.07'12

ISBN 0-340-49173-6

First published 1989

Cover illustration by David Eyre

Typeset in Gill Sans by Taurus Graphics, Abingdon, Oxon.
Printed and bound in Great Britain for Hodder and Stoughton Educational, a division of Hodder and Stoughton Ltd, Mill Road, Dunton Green, Sevenoaks, Kent by St Edmundsbury Press Ltd, Bury St Edmunds, Suffolk

Flightpath

Kes – *The Play*. Well, what happens in it? Billy's home. A paper round. Home. A visit to the local library. Home. School. More school. Home. A trip to the shops. School again. Then home. Nothing out of the ordinary. Hardly remarkable.

Maybe watching a kestrel, drunkenness and a fight in the playground are not such ordinary events, but even they are not really exceptional. No, **Kes**, unlike many plays, does not set out to tell an unusual story. It simply presents a main character, Billy, living his life in a familiar environment where familiar things happen: at home, in school and on 'The Estate'.

The plot is made up of a series of these familiar happenings, loosely connected – all these happenings, or *episodes*, build up our understanding of Billy's situation. Look at the map below: what does it tell you about Billy's life? The same locations for

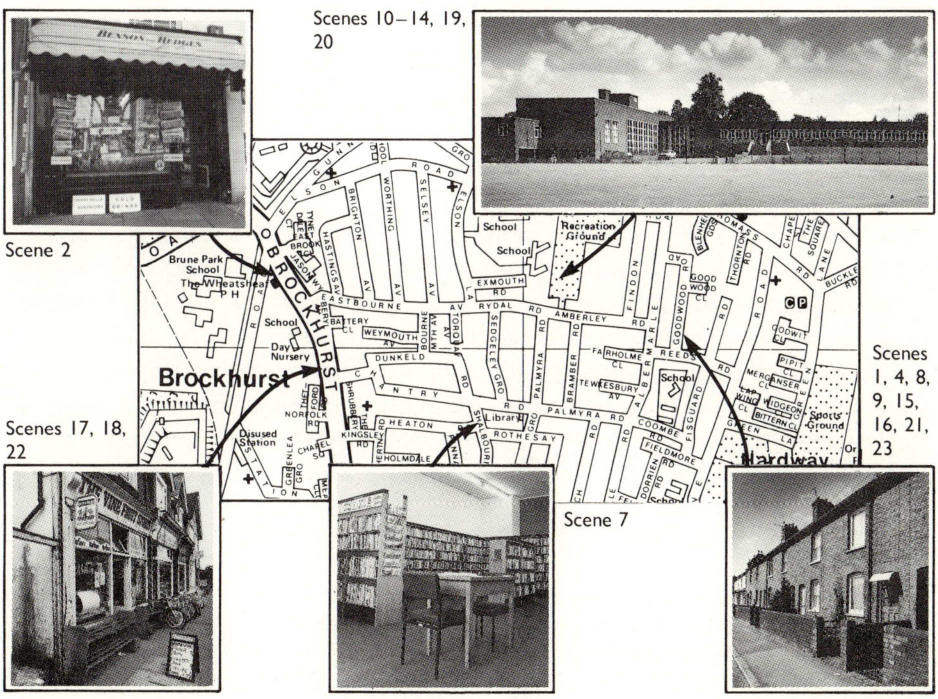

Scenes 10–14, 19, 20

Scene 2

Scenes 1, 4, 8, 9, 15, 16, 21, 23

Scenes 17, 18, 22

Scene 7

episodes in the play are used repeatedly: his house, which he shares with his mother, Mrs Casper, and his half-brother, Jud, his school, where he is seen constantly in and out of trouble and the surrounding estate represented by newsagent, bookmaker and butcher.

It is this physical environment which in part determines Billy's attitudes and behaviour; it is what shapes and moulds him as a person. It is therefore important that the play makes us understand what home, school and estate are like.

Home

At home, there is obviously little comfort and not much money. Billy and Jud share a bed. Jud drains the morning teapot leaving none for Billy. Hungry, Billy resorts to eating Jud's forgotten 'snap'. Housekeeping is obviously difficult, a source of irritation and worry:

Mrs Casper Do me a favour love, and run to the shop for some cigarettes.

Billy They'll not be open yet.

Mrs Casper You can go to the back door. Mr Hardy'll not mind.

Billy I can't. I'll be late.

Mrs Casper Go on love, bring a few things back with you.

Billy Go yourself.

Mrs Casper I've no time. Just tell him to put it in the book and I'll pay him at the weekend.

Billy He says you can't have anything until you've paid up.

Mrs Casper resorts to threatening violence because she has failed to get her own way. We see that home is an unwelcoming place for Billy to live: not only is there Mrs Casper's and Jud's bullying, but there is loneliness. When he stays at home alone at night to read *A Falconer's Handbook* his mother shows no concern over leaving him, but simply provides a kind of 'bribe': '*10p to buy some pop or crisps or something*'. The end of the play repeats this emphasis on Billy's loneliness: when the family gathers together at home the anger directed at Billy arises from the loss of a £13 win on the horses. Kes's death is ignored.

School

The school environment is no more hospitable. Mr Gryce's lack of understanding is expressed, like Mrs Casper's, in the threat of physical violence:

Mr Gryce As far as I can see there's been no advance at all in discipline, decency, manners or morals. And do you know how I know this? Because I still have to use this every day. *(He takes the cane from the top of his desk.)* I can understand why we had to use it back in the twenties and thirties. Those were hard times, they bred hard people and it needed hard measures to deal with them. We knew where we stood in those days; they bred people with respect for a start. Even today a man will stop me in the street and say – 'Hello Mr Gryce, remember me?' And we'll pass away the time of day and he'll laugh about the thrashings I used to give him.

We see that school is harsh, and that Billy can expect little help: even an innocent messenger can be made to leave the room crying.

Violence pursues Billy throughout the day at school. At breaktime he is the victim of MacDowall's bullying. Later, Mr Sugden picks on him, verbally at first:

Mr Sugden Casper. You make me SICK. Every lesson it's the same old story. 'Please Sir, I've got no kit.' Every lesson for five years! And in all that time you've made no attempt whatsoever to get any kit. You've skyved and scrounged and borrowed and . . . Why is it that everyone else can get some, but you can't.

Then, physically, as Sugden hits him with the ball.

By the time the school day ends, Jud has chased Billy around the school whilst Mr Gryce has hit out for a second time.

'The Estate'

It is only when he is out in 'The Estate' that Billy is able to feel any sense of acceptance, of belonging to his environment.

Mr Porter, although he claims that the '*grand lads*' from Firs Hill are queuing up for Billy's paper round, is not really presented as being against him. The milkman stops to pass the time of day with Billy when he sees him. And if his reception at the Public Library is a little frosty, this is not the case when he visits Mr Beal the butcher:

Mr Beal You've still got that bird then?

Billy Yes.

Mr Beal (*wraps the meat up*): Here, you can have that.

Billy For nothing?

Mr Beal They're only scraps.

Billy Thanks. Do you want another chip?

Mr Beal No, I'll be going for my dinner in a bit.

Billy Cheerio, then.

Mr Beal So long.

Yet only five of the episodes in the play take place out in 'The Estate'. You can see this by looking at the map on page 3. Fifteen episodes take place at home or in school. These places therefore provide the strongest impressions we are given of Billy's environment.

Examine your own physical environment. What do you see? Is it urban, a town or city, or rural, the countryside? Do you feel it is welcoming and that you enjoy living in it? What do you like about it? What don't you like about it? The writers Charles Dickens and George Orwell write here of their impressions of the industrial North. Dickens describes it as it appeared to him in the 1850s, Orwell describes the scene he saw in the 1930s. Both men use description to convey the harshness, grimness and overall poverty they experienced in this part of the country; as a result we don't need to hear the people speak to know what their lives are like:

It was a town of red brick, or of brick that would have been red if the smoke and ashes had allowed it; but, as matters stood it was a town of unnatural red and black like the painted face of a savage. It was a town of machinery and tall chimneys, out of which interminable serpents of smoke trailed themselves for ever and ever, and never got uncoiled. It had a black canal in it, and a river that ran purple with ill-smelling dye, and vast piles of buildings full of windows where there was a rattling and a trembling all day long, and where the piston of the steam-engine worked monotonously up and down, like the head of an elephant in a state of melancholy madness. It contained several large streets all very like one another, and many small streets still more like one another, inhabited by people equally like one another, who all went in and out at the same hours, with the same sound upon the same pavements, to do the same work, and to whom every day was the same as yesterday and tomorrow, and every year the counterpart of the last and the next.

Hard Times (1854) Charles Dickens

As you travel northward your eye, accustomed to the South or East, does not notice much difference until you are beyond Birmingham . . . It is only when you get a little further north, to the pottery towns and beyond, that you begin to encounter the real ugliness of industrialism – an ugliness so frightful and so arresting that you are obliged, as it were, to come to terms with it.

I remember a winter afternoon in the dreadful *environs* of Wigan. All round was the lunar landscape of slag-heaps, and to the north, through the passes, as it were, between the mountains of slag, you could see the factory chimneys sending out their plumes of smoke . . . It seemed a world from which vegetation had been banished; nothing existed except smoke, shale, ice, mud, ashes and foul water. But even Wigan is beautiful compared with Sheffield . . . One scene especially lingers in my mind. A frightful patch of waste ground (somehow, up there a patch of waste ground attains a squalor that would be impossible even in London) trampled bare of grass and littered with newspapers and old saucepans. To the right an isolated row of gaunt four-roomed houses, dark red, blackened by smoke. To the left an interminable vista of factory chimneys, chimney beyond chimney, fading away into a dim blackish haze. Behind me a railway embankment made of the slag from furnaces.

At night, when you cannot see the hideous shapes of the houses and the blackness of everything, a town like Sheffield assumes a kind of sinister magnificence. Sometimes the drifts of smoke are rosy with sulphur, and

serrated flames, like circular saws, squeeze themselves out beneath the cowls of the foundry chimneys. Through the open doors of foundries you see fiery serpents of iron being hauled to and fro by red lit boys, and you hear the whizz and thump of steam hammers and the scream of the iron under the blow.

The Road to Wigan Pier (1937) George Orwell

Describe your own area in a similar manner. Concentrate on bringing out not only the sights and sounds but also the atmosphere of where you live.

How do you imagine Billy's home town? Write a description of his street, possibly as it would appear at two different times of day. For example, you could, to match the play, describe it first thing in the morning as Billy leaves home for his paper round. Then, the same scene, but this time in the evening.

Billy talks about Kes

Billy is fidgeting in an English lesson; Mr Farthing has invited Anderson to tell the class something about himself, a fact, something of interest. Somewhat unwillingly, Anderson begins to tell the class about 'taddies', Wellingtons and Reggie Clay. Billy is not listening to him. Mr Farthing, exasperated, threatens to punish the whole class unless . . .

And in this way Billy is forced into telling the story of Kes. At first he begins slowly. Then his enthusiasm for Kes starts to show. And interest grows. He gains confidence. He surprises both himself and his teacher. When he ends, the class applauds, captivated. His talk has been a great success.

Why? Most importantly, he is talking about a subject which deeply interests him. He knows about training hawks from first-hand experience:

I started training Kes when I'd had him about a fortnight.

Excitingly, he is skilled enough with Kes to take important steps on his own:

So while he was feeding I got hold of his jesses.

And he conveys his own genuine enthusiasms:

I was that pleased I didn't know what to do with myself.

Billy's talk is given impromptu, without any preparation. Yet it is fluent and interesting because Billy is simply describing out loud something which normally absorbs his thoughts: his private life, which he is rarely given the opportunity to share. It is quite difficult to give a talk on the spot without any preparation; Billy's success shows how deeply he is involved with Kes.

oral

You can try giving the class an impromptu talk for yourself. Stand up now and give a short talk on a subject that interests you. It may be less easy than you thought! That is why most talks are carefully prepared. Preparation ensures that the talk is clear, fluent and informative, so that the audience is kept interested. This requires the speaker to:

Select
Sort
Structure
Supplement

Select	Like Billy, choose a subject which interests you and which you know about. Spend time on a brain storm. Write down *everything* you can think of to do with your subject. If need be, go away and come back for a second 'go'.
Sort	Look closely at your notes. Group similar ideas together. Arrange as topics.
Structure	Work out a topic order. Add and/or delete ideas. Once sorted, reduce to a minimum. Aim for single 'prompt' words. Write these out neatly on card.
Supplement	Decide on visual aids – illustrations, hand-outs, additional material.

If Billy had prepared his talk, then his preparations might look as follows. Rough notes looking like this:

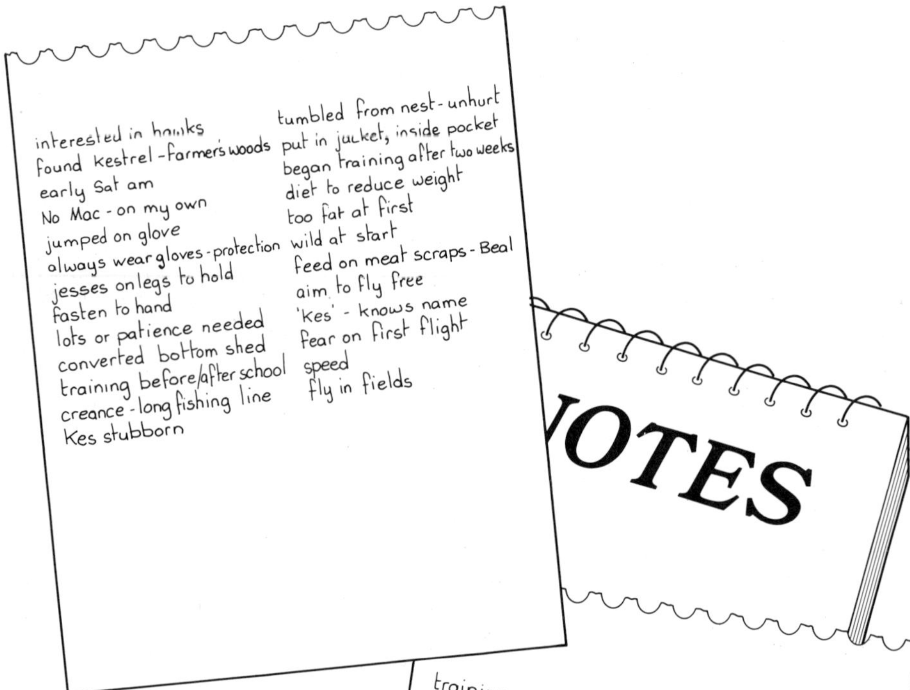

Can be 'sorted' like this:

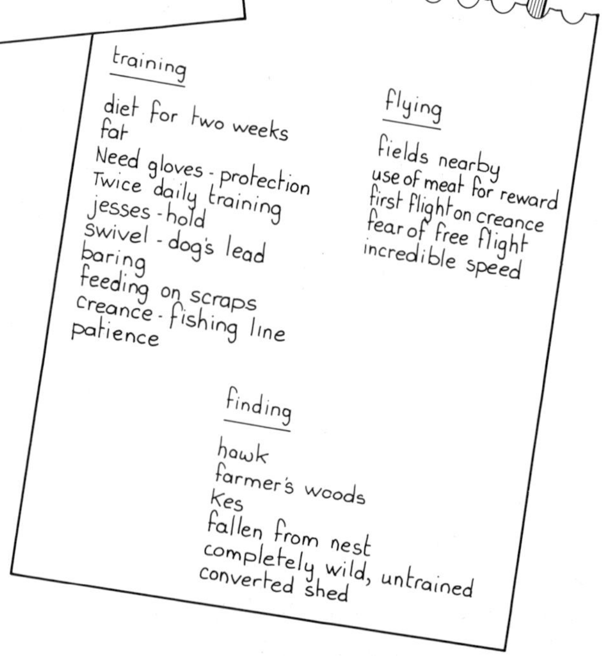

Prepare a talk on a subject which interests you, using the approach described above. Your talk should last for four to five minutes. Make sure you know your notes very well, so that you don't need to refer to them constantly. Try to use at least one visual aid. Put your sorted notes onto neat file cards, as shown in the illustration at the top of the facing page.

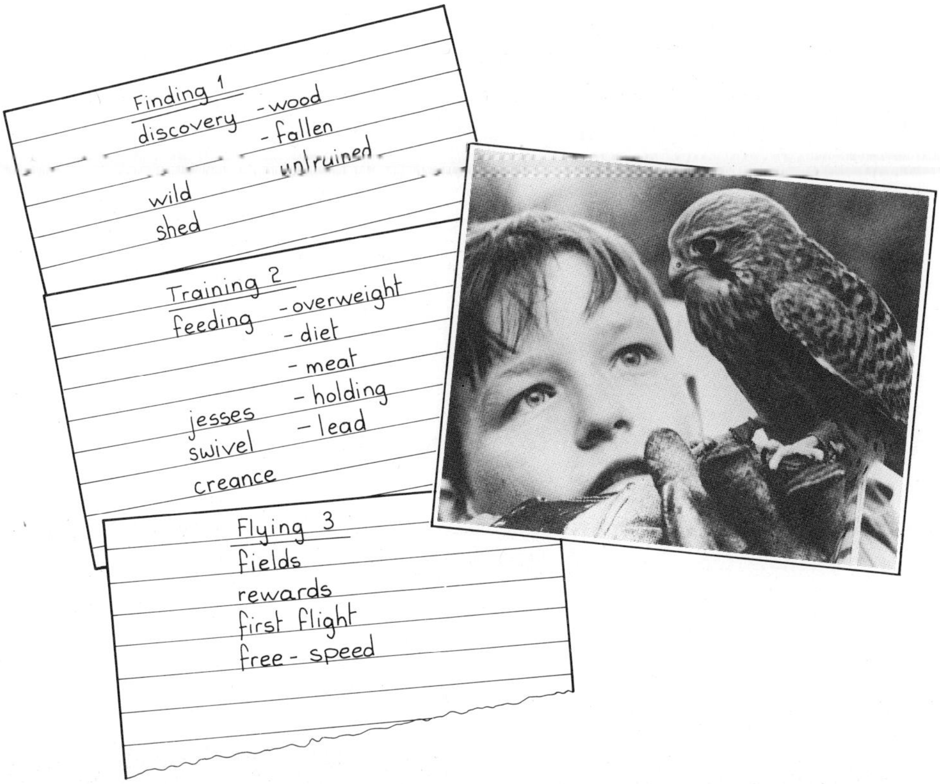

Was your audience interested? Mr Farthing is clearly interested in Billy's talk. His interest does not end with the lesson. During the lunch hour he visits Kes's hut where Billy is checking that Kes is all right.

Mr Farthing Casper.

Billy (*quietly*) Bloody hell fire.

Mr Farthing Can I have a look?

Billy 'Course. Not too close though sir, he's nervous today. Don't know why.

Mr Farthing Beautiful isn't it? Do you know, this is the first time I've really been close to a hawk.

What impresses Mr Farthing is Billy's knowledge, expertise and professional handling of Kes. To promote Billy, and to gain for him some recognition, Mr Farthing contacts the local press.

Immediate interest. A journalist is sent to interview Billy. You are the journalist and you plan to write a feature article in the weekly paper on Billy's story. You must devise a series of questions to ask him. When your questions are ready, persuade a friend, acting as Billy, to supply answers.

Now for your presentation. This could take you to Fleet Street! How about a double page spread? Use the information acquired from your interview as the basis of your story. You will also need to refer to Mr Farthing. What else might be useful?

A map of where Kes was found.
Mrs Casper's reactions.
Details of Kes's training.
Mr Beal's comments.
Pictures: Kes; Billy; Mr Farthing; the farmer.
Technical explanations: jesses; swivel; creance.

In addition, include a few local advertisements. Both Mr Beal and Mr Porter could well buy space.

On the day of publication your double page is spotted by Alex Weston, City Sound's Number One Presenter. Just the thing to slot in on Friday night's programme of music, regional events and happenings. Devise, make and tape the piece about Billy and Kes. Your aim is to make it the most interesting item in the programme.

Billy without Kes

The radio feature about Billy could be put together so as to give the impression that Billy is triumphing over his difficulties and training his hawk. The play, and the novel, by contrast, show the audience that Billy is beaten by circumstances. Read the final stage directions of the play: is there any hope here for Billy?

Lights fade down. Billy walks on. He takes Kes from inside his jacket, kneels down and digs a hole with his hands. He places Kes in the hole and covers it with soil. Fade to blackout.

Compare this with the last paragraph of the novel:

When he arrived home there was no-one in. He buried the hawk in the field just behind the shed; went in, and went to bed.

The play has to show on stage what the novel describes: the impression that with Kes's death something has ended for Billy and he is left to face his everyday world with no help, no private world of interest and challenge. Both the play and the novel end on a solemn note. There are differences, however, between what the play shows us just before the end and what the novel tells us. The play concludes with a violent and angry scene in which Billy confronts his mother and Jud even though it is hopeless. The novel takes Billy, quietly and on his own, to The Palace, a deserted, disused cinema. The way it is described adds to our sense of Billy's hopelessness.

THE PALACE. The arabesque lettering still visible in the plaster above the doorway. The architecture of the façade of Graeco-Arabian inspiration. The doorway was crescent-shaped, the supposed entrance to a cave, and directly above it the crown of the façade described the same curve. At either side pillars had been superimposed on to the wall, and rose to turrets flanking the crown. The whole façade had been finished in plaster, the pillars fluted, but these, like other areas of the façade were peeling, revealing the same brick foundation. The Forthcoming Attractions board advertised nothing. An expanding gate barred the entrance, but failed to cover the upper curve of the doorway, and in the foyer behind the gate lay half bricks and stones, which had been lobbed over at the boarded doors and paybox.

Then we are told about Billy's thoughts: he is still fantasising about his private life as a hero with Kes:

The Pictures. Warm. Full. Smoky. Big Picture. Billy as hero. Billy on the screen. Big Billy. Kes on his arm. Big Kes. Close up. Technicolor. Looking round, looking down on them all, fierce-eyed. Audience murmuring, Billy in the audience, looking round at them all, proud. Billy and Kes on Moor Edge, moor stretching away, empty moor. Billy casting Kes off, flying low, one rapid wide circuit, then gaining height, ringing up, hovering and sliding sideways a few yards, then ringing up to her pitch and waiting on while Billy walks forward . . .

d Use this abandoned cinema as the setting for an additional scene in the play. Of course, you will need to introduce other characters into this new location. Who these characters will be depends on how you want your scene to show Billy's sadness and loneliness. Will he meet someone who gives him help and hope for the future? Or perhaps everything that happens only emphasises his misery and isolation? Work out your ideas. Perhaps Jud follows Billy. A fight could break out. The police intervene? Perhaps the cinema is home for a tramp, and Billy confides his misery, is given some advice. The possibilities are many and varied.

Now write your extra scene as a play script. Include detailed stage directions. When you have finished, act out these original endings to **Kes** in groups.

The play as it is written by Barry Hines and Allan Stronach tells us that for Billy any form of escape must be confined to his imagination. In reality, tomorrow he must face another day with a brutal Jud and an unsympathetic Mrs Casper. The difference now is that he no longer has the comfort of Kes.

d Improvise the scene which takes place first thing next day in Billy's home.

Sparrows and Sparrowhawks

Just look at the people who surround Billy. They represent the *human environment*. Their attitudes to Billy and to each other contribute a great deal towards his development.

Although portrayed as 'cartoon' characters, the people in Billy's life are easily recognised from this design. After all, they are presented to us not so much as individuals but as types. And as such, their characteristics tend to be typical: a bully. An unsympathetic headmaster.

In the box below are written a number of words which could be used to describe these central characters surrounding Billy. Which words would you use to label each character? Why?

conceited sympathetic feckless
cruel patronising heartless tactless
understanding appreciative vindictive
mean selfish unthinking violent
kind
helpful inadequate callous tactful unkind
sensitive harsh unsympathetic
insensitive self-centred aggressive

Many of the words do seem to fit more than one character. What does this tell us about the people in the play? If you could select one word only for each character, which would you choose? Say why?

Who do you think has the greatest influence upon your life? Most would say parents or guardians. In Billy's case, his mother.

Billy's mother

What kind of a woman is she? What sort of example does she set? What does Billy learn from her?

The play tells us that she does not care about her son. She does not appear in the first scene, even though it is at home, at breakfast time. When we do meet her Billy has already completed his paper round. Her first words to him are: '*Haven't you gone to school yet?*'. But there is no concern or urgency in her question. Rather, her immediate concern is for herself, for cigarettes: '*You've not got a fag on you have you?*'

That Billy, who is about fifteen, should smoke is not exceptional. That his mother, as a parent, should encourage him, is.

The play continues to show us that Mrs Casper's interest is centred on herself. When Jud bullies Billy she merely complains: '*You're a couple of noisy buggers.*' When she makes this remark she is on her way out of the house for the evening.

Her shoes are unpolished and her stockings laddered. Still, as she says: '*it'll soon be dark.*' We see that her lack of physical care for her son extends to herself.

She lacks the ability to show any emotional care. She does not encourage Billy to fulfil his potential, does not know how to show oven affection:

Mrs Casper What are you going to do with yourself tonight love?

Billy Read my book.

Mrs Casper That's nice. What's it about?

Billy Falconry. I'm going to get a young kestrel and train it.

Mrs Casper That's nice. I say, what time is it?

Billy offers her the opportunity to talk about his interest in falconry and his ambitions to train a kestrel; Mrs Casper ignores the invitation. Her lack of interest later becomes utterly heartless, desperately wounding and openly cruel:

But it's only a bird. You can get another can't you?

Why does she behave like this? Perhaps the pressures of her life are too much for her. She is trying to bring up two teenagers, alone. There is not much money. Maybe she feels that life is passing her by.

d Script a scene in which Mrs Casper confides in a friend. They could be having a night out together at the pub. She is fed up with Jud and Billy's constant fighting. Billy is doing badly at school. Jud is continually coming home drunk. Her boyfriend has left her. She feels life is fairly hopeless. Her friend tries to help.

Different from Mrs Casper is Mr Farthing. He recognises Billy's potential. He encourages his talent. His interest in Billy is genuine.

Billy's Teachers

Study the English lesson scene. Note the way Mr Farthing involves Billy. He has the ability to persuade Billy to give of his best. His approach to the boys is a direct contrast to that of his colleagues, Mr Gryce and Mr Sugden. He is more relaxed, more patient, more sure of himself.

But he is not totally different. Consider:

Casper. Tibbut. You'll both be asleep in a minute. I'll knock you to sleep.

---

or:

I'm giving you lot ten seconds to get back to the yard. If I see one face after that time, I'll give its owner the biggest beating he's ever had.

What kind of a man is this? On the one hand he appears understanding, even kind, and yet on the other he is clearly capable of physical force.

d Imagine the scene in which Mr Farthing returns tired to the staff room and complains that Billy and MacDowall have been fighting. Mr Gryce and Mr Sugden join in his complaints and they decide that the boys should be taught a lesson. Billy and MacDowall are sent for. Act this out.

Do you think that, in the end, all teachers are alike? Make a list of all the things that *you* would expect the ideal teacher to be, and do. How do Mr Gryce, Mr Sugden and Mr Farthing measure up? Why do you think Mr Farthing can both be interested in Billy and yet at times complain about him like the others?

Think back to a lesson you have experienced. It may be a recent one, or it may be one you remember from your primary school days. Whichever, choose one that is memorable, one that you can write about in vivid detail. Perhaps something strange, unusual or funny happened. It could be that the lesson went very wrong; the teacher made a mistake, an accident happened.

To begin with, write about the lesson as *you* remember it. Include a description of the moods and attitudes of everyone involved: you, your friends, your teacher.

Now paint a 'word picture' of a teacher. You can describe a 'real life' teacher, (do *not* mention real names!) or you can imagine a character. The following extract from Laurie Lee's *Cider with Rosie* is a 'word picture' of Miss B, a junior school teacher. Try and use a similar style of writing in your piece of work.

Each morning was war without declaration; no one knew who would catch it next. We stood to attention, half-crippled in our desks, till Miss B walked in, whacked the walls with a ruler, and fixed us with her squinting eye. 'Good a-morning, children!' 'Good morning, Teacher!' The greeting was like a rattling of swords. Then she would scowl at the floor and begin to growl 'Ar Farther . . .'; at which we said the Lord's Prayer, praised all good things, and thanked God for the health of our King. But scarcely had we bellowed the last Amen than Crabby coiled, uncoiled and sprang, and knocked some poor boy sideways.

One seldom knew why; one was always off guard, for the punishment preceded the charge. The charge, however, followed hard upon it, to a light shower of angry spitting.

'Shuffling your feet! Playing with the desk! A-smirking at that miserable Betty! I will not have it. I'll not, I say. I repeat – I will not have it!'

Many a punch-drunk boy in a playground battle, outnumbered and beaten to his knees, would be heard to cry: 'I will not have it! I'll not, I say! I repeats I will not have it!' It was an appeal to the code of our common suffering, and called for immediate mercy.

Cider with Rosie (1959) Laurie Lee

Now consider the teacher's view of the pupils. D. H. Lawrence knew what it was like to be an unsuccessful teacher. His poem, 'Last Lesson of the Afternoon', draws on his own experiences.

Last Lesson of the Afternoon

When will the bell ring, and end this weariness?
How long have they tugged the leash, and strained apart,
My pack of unruly hounds! I cannot start
Them again on a quarry of knowledge they hate to hunt,
I can haul them and urge them no more.

No longer now can I endure the brunt
Of the books that lie out on the desks; a full three-score
Of several insults of blotted pages, and scrawl
Of slovenly work that they have offered me.
I am sick, and what on earth is the good of it all?
What good to them or me, I cannot see!

So, shall I take
My last dear fuel of life to heap on my soul
And kindle my will to a flame that shall consume
Their dross of indifference; and take the toll
Of their insults in punishment – I will not! –

I will not waste my soul and my strength for this.
What do I care for all that they do amiss!
What is the point of this teaching of mine, and of this
Learning of theirs? It all goes down the same abyss.

What does it matter to me, if they can write
A description of a dog, or if they can't?
What is the point? To us both, it is all my aunt!
And yet I'm supposed to care, with all my might.

I do not, and will not; they won't and they don't; and that's all!
I shall keep my strength for myself; they can keep theirs as well.
Why should we beat our heads against the wall
Of each other? I shall sit and wait for the bell.

D. H. Lawrence

Lawrence sees his pupils as a 'pack of unruly hounds' who have no wish to learn anything. Their work is reduced to 'insults of blotted pages'. At the end of the afternoon he finds himself questioning the point of his 'teaching' and their 'learning'. He resigns himself simply to sitting and waiting for the bell.

As a close observer of this particular lesson, perhaps as a school inspector, write a detailed report of all that you see. Structure your work to include:

1 setting: class, number of pupils, teacher, subject, period, date, time;
2 observations: teacher (attitude, approach, interest, etc.);
pupils (behaviour, involvement, etc.); and
3 recommendations: ways in which situation could be improved.

Billy will shortly leave school. Does anyone at the school really know anything about him? A visit to the Youth Employment Officer reveals that he knows little of Billy's personality. This is not entirely his fault. The interview is brief. Billy is uncommunicative, unconcerned and uninterested.

Before his interview Billy will have been asked to complete a Careers Form. Most likely he will not have done this. It is not difficult to imagine the Careers Service requesting more information on Billy from his headmaster at school.

The Shires Education Committee
The Castle
Northton

19 March 1968

The Headmaster,
Mr W Gryce
The Estate Comprehensive School
Anytown
Midlandshire

Dear Sir,

As you will be aware, we have arranged for our Employment Officer to meet Billy Casper (5-D) next Wednesday afternoon to discuss his future employment when he leaves school at Easter.

Billy has so far failed to complete his Careers Form so we should welcome your comments concerning his suitability for employment. In particular, we should be grateful for information about his character, reliability, honesty, academic ability, interests, both inside and outside school, relationship with others, work experience and home background. Naturally this information will be treated with strict confidence.

We look forward to hearing from you.

Yours faithfully,

S Worsley.

Youth Employment Officer

Here is Mr Gryce's reply. It is, perhaps, typical of the reaction of most of Billy's teachers. Can you say in what ways it says more about Mr Gryce than it does about Billy?

The Shires Education Committee

The Headma
Mr W Gryce
The Estate C
Anytown
Midlandshire

Dear Sir,

As you w
to meet Billy
employment

Billy has
welcome you
particular, we
reliability, ho
outside scho
background.
confidence.

We look

Billy Jasper - 59

Billy Jasper is a boy about whom I have little of good to say

He is a boy who is frequently in trouble, who requires strong discipline and who has a tendency to lie. His behaviour in school leaves much tobe desired and he has been frequently reported to me as a trouble maker

His school work isof a poor standard.His form master, Mr. Crossly, reports a silly attitude whilst in most subjects he fails to produce work. He showsno interest in Physical Education although he has received much encouragement from his games master, Mr. Sugden.

As far asI am aware, he has no outside interests although he does have a job as a paper boy.

Billy casper has fewfriends and is frequently to be found fighting. He is disruptive in the classroom.

Although Billy comes from a one-parent family, both his mother and elder brother take a keeninterest in his school life. A very supportive home background.

Now write the report as if it were written by Mr Farthing.

The reference from Mr Gryce and the school report tell us what the teachers think of Billy. But what about the other way round? What does he think of his teachers? Possibly he would have most to say about Mr Sugden. About his bullying tactics and sarcasm.

Martin I hate P.E. with him. It's always football. This weather as well.

Allen We haven't been in the Gym for years now.

Martin Other classes do basketball sometimes.

Allen Where is he anyway? Is he here today?

Martin Oh he'll be here all right. He wouldn't miss double football for anything.

SUGDEN *runs into the changing room and twice round it.*

Mr Sugden Right lads. No time for shirking. Let's have you changed. Changed and out. You should be pushing at the door fully kitted up shouting, 'Let's get out sir, to the field, to the field'. (BILLY *enters*) Skyving again Casper?

Billy No sir, Mr Farthing wanted me – he's been talking to me.

Mr Sugden I bet that was stimulating for him, wasn't it?

Billy What does that mean sir?

Mr Sugden The conversation, lad, what do you think it means?

Billy No sir, that word, stimu . . . stimu . . . la . . . tin.

Mr Sugden Stimulating you fool s-t-i-m-u-l-a-t-i-n-g stimulating.

Billy Yes sir.

Mr Sugden Well get changed lad – you're two weeks late already. (*Looks at watch*) Some of us want a game even if you don't.

Consider this too:

Mr Sugden Shut up lad! Shut up, before you drive me crackers. (*He hits him with the ball twice. He goes into his room and brings out a giant pair of drawers*) Here Casper, get them on. (*He throws them at* BILLY)

Billy They'll not fit me sir. (*The class laugh*)

Mr Sugden What are you talking about lad. You can get them on, can't you?

Billy Yes sir.

Mr Sugden Well they fit you then. Now get changed. Quick.

Both extracts give ample reasons for Billy's dislike of his games teacher.

This time, imagine that you are Billy. Write a story called 'The Games Lesson' from your point of view. Describe what happened, your feelings and what you thought of Sugden's behaviour.

Does Billy have friends?

Billy seems to be something of a loner, preferring his own company or that of Kes. True, there is MacDowall. They do arrange to go bird nesting together but MacDowall is unreliable. He lets him down by staying in bed. Billy goes alone.

After that they do not have much time for each other. They quarrel and fight. MacDowall shows himself to be a loud mouth and a bully.

Billy is none too popular with his class. It seems there is quite a lot of feeling against him. As Tibbut says:

He never comes out with anybody else now, he just looks after this hawk.

---

oral

Do you think this is a cause for his classmates to resent him? What other reasons could you suggest for Billy's unpopularity?

At Billy's age, whatever we may pretend, we all want to be liked. Billy is no exception. In the novel, he proves this when he writes his 'tall story'.

A tall story

One day I wolke up and my muther said to me heer Billy theres your brecfast in bed for you there was backen and egg and bred and butter and a big pot of tea when I had my brekfast the sun was shining out side and I got drest and whent down stairs we lived in a big hous up moor edge and we add carpits on the stairs and in the all and sentrall eeting. When I got down I said wers are Jud his goind the army my muther saide and hees not coming back. but your dades coming back in sted. there was a big fire in the room and my dad came in caring his cas that he tulke a way with him I havent seen him for a long time but he was just the sam as he went away I was glad hed come back and are Jud had gon away when I got to school all the teacherr were good to me they said allow Billy awo you gowing on and they all pated me on the head and smilled and we did interesting things all day.when I got home my muther saide I not gowing to work eny more and we all had chips beans for awur tea then we got redy and we all went to the picturs we went up stairs and had Ice cream at the intervells and then we all went home and had fish and chips for awur super and then we went to bed.

Although intended to be made up, it does tell us a great deal about Billy's private hopes and dreams: Mrs Casper cares. Jud, ever ready with his fists, is removed to the army. The house is warm. The family is once more complete. At school Billy becomes a centre of interest; at home there is plentiful food, and treats.

Billy's 'tall story' tells us about a 'happy' day. Yet it is a pathetic picture. Can you say in what ways? Why does the story invite our pity?

For all of this, Billy is a survivor. Somehow he will come through. The day will come when Billy will look back, perhaps not with nostalgia but neither with bitterness. He may even laugh.

Fifteen years on. Billy, now thirty, recalls that last year at school. He writes about it:

I remember

I must have just turned fifteen. It was winter time, cold and pitch dark. Mining mornings! Jud, a half drunk pig, would ...

Continue his story.

Home to Roost

Study this picture. What do you see? Look for a second time. Are the three figures the same height? Measure them and see!

So it is with **Kes**. On the surface, it is a portrayal of the everyday life of a boy at home, at school, a boy who is interested in training a kestrel. But if we look more closely, something more is revealed about this everyday life.

Consider the world which Billy inhabits. A familiar but disturbing world. **A world of no respect for others** where the individual, whether a family member or not, is treated to verbal and physical abuse, where women are treated as objects and where differences of opinion are settled by force.

Billy You'll be late.

Jud Oh, shut it.

Billy Clock's gone off you know.

Jud I said 'shut it'! (*He thumps Billy*)

Jud I'm hoping I'll be laid watching a bird tonight, but she won't have feathers on.

MacDowall Get away you squirt, before I spit on you and drown you. (*Billy rushes at him again and they begin to fight.*)

A world of limited opportunity where people are pushed into jobs, where potential is wasted and where horizons are narrowed rather than widened.

Billy Just think, when I'm doing 'papers you'll be going down the cage.

Jud Yeh. And just think, in a few weeks you'll be coming down wi'me.

Gryce And God help anyone who employs you.

Youth Employment Officer . . . and if you can stand a hard day's graft and not mind getting dirty, then there are good opportunities in mining.

A world of prejudice where ideas are formed and opinions expressed which are based on ignorance and not on fact.

Mr Porter You know what they said when I took you on don't you? They said – 'you'll have to keep your eyes open now, you know, 'cos they're all alike off that estate. They'll take your breath if you're not careful.'

A world of materialism where money is valued more highly than feelings and emotions.

Jud Win? I'd have had £13 to draw if he'd kept his thieving hands to himself.

Mrs Casper £13? Billy, you've done it once too often this time.

Jud £13. I could have had a few days off work with that. I'd have bloody killed him if I'd have got hold of him this afternoon.

Mrs Casper What's he crying about then?

Billy Because he's killed my hawk instead, that's why.

A world of misunderstanding in which assumptions are made and judgements pronounced without giving thought to the truth.

Gryce Don't know? You wouldn't be tired if you got to bed at night instead of sitting up till dawn watching some tripe on television.

In fact, Billy's everyday world is not presented as an 'ordinary' background to the main story; rather it is shown to be a world which is severely lacking, one which disregards things we believe to be important. Things like truth, loyalty, selflessness, caring, self-esteem, understanding. The nature of Billy's world is an essential part of the story.

Billy's world and ours

How does this affect *us*? Billy's world, as we see it in **Kes**, affects us because in looking at it more closely we are, in fact, also being asked to look at and question our own world.

What is our world really like?
Our homes?
Our schools?
Our society?
Our values?

The attitudes to life observed in **Kes** often closely resemble those to be found around us in our everyday lives.
How does Billy cope with his world? He has Kes. In Kes he finds something he recognises as being of value. Something more satisfying than the concerns of his

daily life. For Kes is not simply a hawk. It is a thing of beauty, of independence, unrestricted by human concerns, fierce, following its own wild instincts in which Billy is to some extent able to share. Indeed, for Billy Kes provides a vision of life with a new depth of meaning.

Make a list of all the things *you* believe to matter and to be of value in your life. Compare your list with a friend's. Discuss differences and similarities.

Escape or change?

Billy 'escapes' from his world. Others might react differently; protest, try to change their lives in some way, cry out for help. In this poem the poet Vernon Scannell describes a young boy, perhaps a little like Billy, who sets fire to 'three thousand guineas worth of property and crops at Godwin's Farm'.

Incendiary

That one small boy with a face like pallid cheese
And burnt-out little eyes could make a blaze
As brazen, fierce and huge, as red and gold
And zany yellow as the one that spoiled
Three thousand guineas worth of property
And crops at Godwin's Farm on Saturday
Is frightening – as fact and metaphor:
An ordinary match intended for
The lighting of a pipe or kitchen fire
Misused may set a whole menagerie
Of flame-fanged tigers roaring hungrily.
And frightening, too, that one small boy should set
The sky on fire and choke the stars to heat
Such skinny limbs and such a little heart
Which would have been content with one warm kiss
Had there been anyone to offer this.

Vernon Scannell

Immediately we sympathise with this boy. His face is pale, expressionless, empty, his eyes deep-set, hollow, even lifeless.

Taking a single match he ignites a fire so fierce and so dangerous that the poet describes it as '*a whole menagerie/Of flame-fanged tigers roaring hungrily.*' The flames are clearly very frightening, lighting up the sky, reaching for the stars. Why has the boy wanted to start such a terrifying fire?

Like Barry Hines and Allan Stronach, the poet is making a point about society. The boy, as Billy, is, or certainly feels, unloved, unwanted, neglected and rejected. His is a cry for help.

Divide into groups. First, consider the boy's circumstances. Make decisions about his home background, his schooling, his attitudes. Secondly, discuss ways in which society can help a boy like this. What solutions are there? Thirdly, the boy is found at the fire. Improvise the events that follow. Include parents, school, the police and social services.

Learning from daily experience

Attitudes that abound in society are important as a theme in **Kes**. So, too, is the way in which Billy is seen to grow up, the way in which he learns from his daily experiences.

As a result of his training of Kes, his dealings with all those around him, he gains. At the end of the play he is more confident as a person, believing a little more in his own abilities. His determination has shown through giving him prized independence. He has learnt, admittedly at a price, that life is hard, often unfair and seldom just.

What other of life's lessons has he learnt? About family? About friends? About school? Pick out extracts from the play to support what you say.

What has life taught *you*? Tell of some experiences you have had which have given you an insight into yourself, human behaviour or the ways of the world.

Write a short story called 'The Discovery' in which a character learns some universal truth.

The problems of others

In many ways people like Billy, Mrs Casper and Jud need understanding, most of all from other people. They join with others, young and old, in cities, towns and villages throughout the country, who are in desperate need of thought and help from family, friends and the society in which they live.

As a member of your local Citizens Advice Bureau, it is your responsibility to carry out a survey aimed at helping people in your area who may be in distress. Before you can do anything you must gather information.

To do so you will require careful preparation and some local research. You cannot include every need you see around you. Decide on priorities: the old, the homeless, the sick. For example, you could concentrate on the needs of old people.

Work in pairs or small groups to carry out your survey. Some suggestions of things to do are listed over the page. You may have ideas of your own. Discuss them with your teacher.

Research plan:

1 Compile a list of all residential homes for the elderly. Divide into categories according to accommodation (single or shared rooms), facilities (TV, private bathroom), charges, night attention, etc.

2 Devise a questionnaire to discover how old people spend their days. Questions might relate to how much time is spent watching television, going out, being alone, etc. If possible, collect answers from as large a number of old people as you can. Show your results in the form of a bar or pie chart.

3 Find out what entertainments are available to old people within your area. Include: music, theatre, cinema, bingo, clubs, societies, sports, etc. Locate them on a map.

4 Survey local shops, libraries, surgeries, pubs, cafes. How many, and which, cater for the old? Do they provide handrails for steps, ramps and space for wheelchairs, lifts, seats, warmth, etc?

4 Now draft simple and attractive information leaflets to circulate to old people, particularly those living alone. What special information would be useful?

How to keep warm on a low budget.
How to protect against intruders.
How to shop economically for nutritious foods.
How to cope with disabilities.
Where to go to meet other people.

In Tune

Study these three snippets of conversation.

Mr Porter Morning Sir. Nice again.

Man Twenty Players please.

Mr Porter Certainly Sir. Thank you.

Billy I want a book on falconry.

Librarian I'm not sure. You'd better try under ornithology.

Billy What's that?

Librarian Under Zoology.

Gryce (*shouting*) And where do you think you've been lad?

Billy Nowhere Sir.

Gryce Nowhere? Don't talk ridiculous lad. Who do you think you are – the invisible man?

What do you notice about them?

Well, to begin with the situations are entirely different. The first takes place in a shop, the second in a library and the third in a school.

> Mr Porter is talking to a customer. He politely greets him, calling him 'Sir'. He is respectful. He comments on the weather. He obliges the customer promptly, again slipping in 'Sir'. He thanks the man.

The librarian is more matter of fact. She refers Billy to a particular section of the library. Tells him to try ornithology, under Zoology. She, doing a professional job of work, uses precise terms.

Mr Gryce is telling Billy off. Calling him 'lad', rather than Billy, makes him more distant, less personal. He repeats Billy's answer to suggest that Billy is stupid. At the same time he calls him 'ridiculous'. He then, in order to put down Billy completely, resorts to sarcasm.

The kind of language we use, the words we choose and the way in which we say and write them, depends on who we are, where we are, and to whom we are talking or writing.

Register

Understanding and appreciating the use of different language styles and vocabulary to suit particular circumstances or subject matter is to know *Register.*

So, what we find in **Kes**, as in our daily lives, are examples of different registers.

Mr Porter, addressing his customers, uses a different register from the one he uses to talk to Billy, the delivery boy.

The librarian, at work, employs a different register from, say, the one used with colleagues during a coffee break.

Mr Gryce, the teacher, tells Billy off in one register. He utilises another, as Headmaster, to speak to the whole school.

Billy himself is no exception to this. At home he uses a variety of registers, all of which are informal. His 'audience' here is Jud and Mrs Casper. The language is ordinary, everyday, sometimes coarse. It matches a situation which lacks any kind of refinement.

At school, with his mates, his choice of language and the way he uses it is much the same or possibly even more informal. To his teachers he adopts a formal register. With them he is careful, guarded, in what he says. He falls in with convention, addressing them as 'Sir'.

Put simply, Billy is doing what we all do: learning to adapt and manipulate language so that we use it to express the different attitudes and roles we take on in daily life.

Think about Mrs Casper as an example. In the course of a day she will speak (if not write) to many different people in a variety of situations. She will talk to:

Billy
Jud
Her neighbour
Mr Hardy
Who else?

Each time she will choose suitable language and quality of expression to fit the occasion. She will be using different registers.

Take yourself. Make a note of all the people you talk to or write to in a typical day. Decide when you are using a formal register, when an informal one.

Register

Formal	Informal
School secretary	Mum
Form teacher	Milkman
Geography homework	Form teacher
Class talk (English)	Friends (in breaktime)

In many situations you will find that you switch from one register to another so that, as we have shown by including the form teacher twice, you will be speaking and writing both formally and informally.

Speaking

Each of these pictures shows people talking:

For each, make up a dialogue picking an appropriate register. Set your work out as direct speech or in play form.

The settings listed below would require a fairly formal register. Choose one and use it as the subject of a group drama sketch. Make your dialogue as realistic and convincing as possible.

The Annual General Meeting of the Youth Club
Hospital – The Casualty Department
An Estate Agent's Office
In Court – The End of the Trial

Now, imagine you are Mr Gryce! You are preparing your speech for the School's Annual Prize Giving. You will select a very formal register for this occasion as you will be addressing distinguished visitors, parents, pupils, staff and friends of the school. You will need to think out very carefully what you are going to say. Your address could contain comments on:

the new building programme,
examination results,
sports achievements,
staff retirements,
news of past pupils,
activities of the PTA,
future plans.

Write the speech!

As a group, make a tape recording of Mrs Casper visiting Billy's school for a Parents' Evening. Concentrate on her talking to a number of different teachers. Use a variety of registers.

Finally, improvisation! Working with friends devise short sketches for one or more of these scenes:

Cinema Foyer
'McDonald's'
Doctor's Surgery
Left Luggage Office
Art Gallery

Don't forget – suitable language!

Writing

In contrast to conversational registers is the manner in which Billy writes in his private diary. This is very informal: the only audience is himself. He writes of his dreams, worries, experiences, Kes, family and so on.

Write a diary as Billy might have done for one day in his life.

Before doing so, you may like to read these extracts from *The Secret Diary of Adrian Mole aged 13¾*.

WEDNESDAY JULY 8TH

My father is near to despair because of Bert's snoring. It doesn't bother me, I put Blu-tack in my ears.

Went to school today. I have decided to take Domestic Science, Art, Woodwork and English O levels. I am doing Geography, Maths and History for CSE.

Pandora is taking nine O levels. But she has had more advantages than me. She has been a member of the library since she was three.

THURSDAY JULY 9TH

School breaks up for eight weeks tomorrow. Pandora is going to Tunisia soon. How I will survive without my love is anybody's guess. We have tried French kissing but neither of us liked it, so we have gone back to the English.

My skin is dead good. I think it must be a combination of being in love and Lucozade.

FRIDAY JULY 10TH

It was magic at school today. All the teachers were in good moods. A rumour went round that pop-eyed Scruton was seen laughing but I didn't believe it myself.

Barry Kent climbed up the flagpole and flew a pair of his mother's knickers in the breeze. Pandora said it was probably the first airing they had had for years.

Sean O'Leary is nineteen today. He has invited me to his birthday party. It is only over the road so I won't have far to go.

I am writing up my diary now just in case I have one too many. People seem to get drunk just stepping over the O'Leary's threshold.

SATURDAY JULY 11TH

First proper hangover. Aged fourteen years, five months and nine days. Pandora put me to bed. She gave me a fireman's lift up the stairs.

Sue Townsend

In the Wings

A play demands much of the imagination. This is particularly so of a play like **Kes**, intentionally episodic, with its twenty-three scenes.

Obviously, in producing **Kes** it is impossible to depict fully on stage all the locations. At best, one or two may be represented – for example, Billy's house. The remainder must rely on suggestion, the use of key props.

So, Mr Porter's shop becomes a table, a pile of newspapers and a pair of steps. Morning Assembly at school is suggested by a lectern. A school corridor requires no more than the actors themselves.

Decide how you would show the following:

Billy meets the milkman	(Scene 3)
The PE changing room	(Scene 14)
The butcher's shop	(Scene 18)

Limit yourself to the bare essentials by way of props. You will quickly discover how little is actually needed. What becomes important is how you imagine and interpret what you see.

One difficulty which has to be faced by the producer of **Kes** is how to present Billy's kestrel. A real bird? A model? On film? Slide projection? Or just imagined? Which do you think would be the most effective of these methods? Why?

Good novel, good play?

Notwithstanding the problems posed by all the locations and the kestrel, **Kes** is successful as a play. This is partly because it has an excellent source – Barry Hines's novel *A Kestrel for a Knave*.

Is it a matter of chance that a good novel will make a good play? No. To adapt one kind of medium to form another requires skill, ingenuity and awareness: how can the new medium convey the ideas shown in the original one?

To help decide if a novel can be adapted to become a good play, we do have certain criteria which are used to measure how well the material can be adapted. Criteria are tests. For **Kes**, these tests could include:

1. **Is the novel well structured?**
(does it have a definite beginning, middle and end?)
2. **Are the characters strong?**
(do they come over as real people living believable lives?)
3. **Are there definite themes?**
(can we recognise ideas and interests of importance?)
4. **Is the dialogue plausible?**
(is what people say true to life?)
5. **Is the setting appropriate?**
(is the background to the novel suitable to become play scenes?)
6. **Does the novel have sufficient appeal?**
(is it of enough interest to keep an audience's attention?)

How does the novel *A Kestrel for a Knave* stand up to these criteria?

1 Barry Hines's novel is well structured. The beginning is Billy in bed:

✓

> Billy moved over, towards the outside of the bed.

The start of a new day. As the day unfolds, so the pattern of Billy's life emerges: paper round, home, a row. Flash to the past: nesting, the library, fighting Jud, Kes. Present: school, day-dreaming, English lesson, playground, P.E. And so until nightfall. The end, much as the start, for we are told Billy 'went to bed'.

2 The characters are strong. Take Billy. We laugh with him:

As Billy squeezed past, he shook the steps and grabbed Porter's legs.

'Look out, Mr Porter!'

Porter sprawled forward into the shelving, his arms spread wide, his fingers scratching for a hold.

'You're all right, I've got you!'

Billy held Porter's legs while he pushed himself off the shelves and regained his balance. His face and bald patch were greasy with sweat.

We admire him:

Billy approached the hawk slowly, regarding it obliquely, clucking and chanting softly, 'Kes Kes Kes.' The hawk bobbed her head and shifted along the perch. Billy held out his gauntlet and offered her a scrap of beef. She reached forward and grasped it with her beak, and tried to pull it from his glove. Billy gripped the beef tightly between forefinger and thumb; and in order to obtain more leverage, the hawk stepped on to his fist. He allowed her to take the beef, then replaced her on the perch, touching the backs of her legs against the wood so that she stepped backwards on to it. He dipped into the leather satchel at his hip and offered her a fresh scrap; this time holding it just out of range of her reaching beak. She bobbed her head and tippled forward slightly, regained balance, then glanced about, uncertain, like someone up on the top board for the first time.

'Come on, Kes. Come on then.'

We pity him:

'Fast asleep during the Lord's Prayer! I'll thrash you, you irreverent scoundrel!'

He demonstrated the act twice down the side of the lectern.

'Were you tired, lad?'

'I don't know, Sir.'

'Don't know? You wouldn't be tired if you'd get to bed at night instead of roaming the streets at all hours up to mischief!'

'No, Sir.'

'Or sitting up 'til dawn watching some tripe on television! Report to my room straight after assembly. You will be tired when I've finished with you, lad!'

We despair of him:

Bloody hell, it's like lead, that ball. It's just like gettin' t'stick across your feet.'
He stood stork fashion and manipulated his foot. Every time he turned his toes up water squeezed into the folds of the instep of his pump.
'Bugger me. I'm not kicking that again.'

We hate with him:

Billy was screaming and crying into Jud's ears.

And we weep for him:

Billy broke from between them, out through the kitchen to the dustbin at the side of the garage. He yanked the lid off and peered down. It was black inside so he reached down, fingers feeling lightly amongst the rubbish. Then he stopped feeling, and straightened up quickly, holding the hawk in his hand.

He carried it into the kitchen and stood with his back to the living-room door to inspect it. Brown eyes open. Glass eyes. Curved beak ajar, tongue just visible in the slit. Head lolling downwards, swinging whichever way he turned it to brush away the dust and ashes from the feathers. Blowing the feathers clean, raising them with his breath, then smoothing them gently into place with his fingers.

Billy's credibility is that he can, and does, arouse such emotions in us.

3 There are definite themes. Attitudes, values, growing up, isolation, hope and despair all present themselves as strong themes. In reading the novel we start to consider these ideas and issues. Our concern rises as we become more involved with the novel.

4 The dialogue is plausible. We can easily imagine this argument developing between Jud and Billy:

'What's tha want that for when tha can't read?'
Jud reached over Billy's shoulder and snatched the book out of his hands.

Billy jumped up from the kitchen step and ran after him into the living-room.

'Giz it back! Come here!'

Jud held him off, tilting his head and trying to read the title at arm's length as the book flapped open and shut.

'Falconry! What's thar know about falconry?'

'Giz it back.'

Jud pushed him back on to the settee, then started to examine the book at leisure.

'*A Falconer's Handbook*. Where's tha got this from?'

'I've lent it.'

'Nicked it, more like. Where's tha got it from?'

'A shop in town.'

'Tha must be crackers.'

'How's tha mean?'

'Nicking books.'

He looked at a picture, then slapped it shut.

'I could understand it if it wa' money, but chuff me, not a book.'

He skimmed it hard across the room. The covers flapped open and when Billy grabbed at it, he bent and scuffled the pages back.

'Look what tha's done now! I'm trying to look after this book.'

He smoothed the bent pages, then shut the covers and squeezed them tight.

'Anybody's think it wa' a treasure tha'd got.'

'It's smashing! I've been reading it all afternoon. I'm nearly half-way through already.'

'An' what better off will tha be when tha's read it?'

'A lot, 'cos I'm goin' to get a young kestrel an' train it.'

'Train it! Tha couldn't train a flea!'

This kind of 'conversation' many of us will have experienced with brothers or sisters at some point. See how readily it converts into play script.

Scene 8 Billy's House

BILLY *is quietly sitting reading the book from the library when* JUD *enters.*

Jud (*getting ready to go out for the night*) What do you want that for, when you can't read? (*Snatches the book from him.*)

Billy Give it me back. Come here.

Jud Falconry? What do you know about falconry?

Billy Give it me back.

Jud *A Falconer's Handbook*. Where have you got this from?

Billy I've lent it.

Jud Nicked it more like. Where have you got it from?

Billy The library in town.

Jud You must be cracked.

Billy How do you mean?

Jud Nicking books. I could understand it if it was money but chuff me, not a book.

Billy I've been reading it all afternoon. I'm nearly halfway through.

Jud And what better off will you be when you've read it?

Billy A lot because I'm going to get a young kestrel and train it.

Jud You couldn't train a flea. Anyroad, where you goin' to get a kestrel from?

---

5 Are the settings appropriate to a stage production?

✓

The living room curtains were drawn, and when he switched the light on it was gloomy and cold without the help of the fire. He placed the clock on the mantelpiece, then picked up his mother's sweater from the settee and pulled it on over his shirt.

It is not difficult to create on stage a cheerless, untidy living room. Nor does a school changing room present any major problems:

He walked into the changing room as clean and shining as a boy down for breakfast on his seaside holidays. The other boys were packed into the aisles between the rows of pegs, their hanging clothes partitioning the room into corridors. Mr Sugden was passing slowly across one end of the room, looking down the corridors and counting the boys as they changed.

In a similar way, this prose . . .

Billy turned the knob and opened the door. At the far end, stretching the width of the room, was a counter, mounted by a wire guard. Benches were situated round the walls and on one wall was a green felt board plastered with racing papers. Only a few strips of green showed between the pages, and from the fireplace directly opposite it looked as though felt scraps had been pinned haphazardly to the sheets. A fire was burning quietly in the grate, and over the mantelpiece, on a calendar, a jockey sat quietly on a quiet grey. In the centre of the room an old kitchen table was littered with more papers, and boxes of clean betting slips, and pencils tied to strings. A man was bending over the table writing, his pencil vertical, its string at full stretch. Another man was seated by the fire studying form, head down, elbows in his thighs, and at the board two men were pointing at the same spot on a page, murmuring and nodding together in consultation. All the men wore caps. Behind the counter a woman was pouring tea from a flask. When she lifted the cup she projected her lips towards it, and the steam made her narrow her eyes.

... can easily be transformed into these stage directions:

Scene 17 Bookmaker's shop *People are sitting around on chairs, some looking at newspapers, some waiting for the next race to begin.* MRS ROSE *is taking bets behind the counter.* BILLY *enters.*

6 Does the novel have sufficient appeal? Well, the modern happenings within it are those we can all relate closely to. Billy's everyday world is, in so many ways, our world too. We identify with Billy, we care about what happens to him.

Applying the criteria

The criteria discussed above are quite general ones. Others will be more specific, dealing with particular episodes and ideas found in the novel. For example:

a How would Mr Gryce act out the cane scene?

b How may the Youth Employment Officer's lack of interest in Billy be shown?

Add to the two questions that we have suggested. When you have done this, answer your queries in the way that we have done in the following examples:

a By placing Mr Gryce with his back to the audience the actual caning need not be seen. Instead, the violence of the scene may be suggested by noise - the whack of the cane, the boy's cries.

b The Youth Employment Officer could remain seated. He need not look at Billy. When Billy is speaking he will be distracted - sorting through papers, writing, even polishing his glasses. He may even keep glancing at his watch.

Behind the bright lights

Whenever the theatre is mentioned we tend to think of bright lights, excitement and glamour. A tour of London's West End, particularly at night, is confirmation of this.

It is seldom that the *Box Office* gets a mention. And yet its role is vital. Not only does the Box Office issue tickets, it is also the centre for much theatre administration.

Suppose you are Press and Marketing Manager in the Box Office of your local theatre. A production of **Kes** is planned. It is up to you to publicise it to schools within the area. You hope to attract large audiences and so you are aiming to produce attractive and informative flyers, tickets and programmes . . .

The *flyer* will be an attractive, colourful leaflet, an essential part of your advertising campaign. It should be designed to appeal to the teachers and students you will be writing to about your theatre's production of **Kes**. Include:

the play's title – **Kes**
the names of the playwrights – Barry Hines and Allan Stronach
the name and address of your theatre – perhaps with 'logo'
names of leading players
performance dates and times
seat prices

Next, a letter to schools. Although set out formally with the layout of a business letter, you should aim to be informative and welcoming.

Q–Players

Head of English
Hampton Park School,
Satchell Lane,
Hemple,
Southampton
SO16 7NV

14 December 1988

Dear Head of English,

I am writing to you about our SPECIAL SCHOOLS' MATINEES for our latest production, 'Kes', Barry Hines and Allan Stronach...

What to write?

Something of interest to schools. Arrangements for two special matinees together with dates, times and, most importantly, special or concessionary seat prices. You will need to give a brief synopsis, to say what the play is about, and include how it will appeal to young people. Why not offer an after show discussion with the cast and director? Do not forget to enclose a booking form.

Following this a *ticket* design will be necessary. Again, the format needs to be clear and eye-catching. Consider only essential information.

Finally, a *programme*. To tempt people to buy one, the cover should be carefully thought out: what attracts you to buy a programme for an event? Do you think the programme cover for **Kes** should have an illustration, a geometrical design or simply typography? It is not only the outside of the programme that attracts people to buy of course. The information inside is very important. You should list the characters in the play and corresponding names of the actors. A chance to cast your favourite television stars? Look at the cast list for the play below. It tells the reader who the characters are, when to expect intervals and how long the play

'Tis Pity She's A Whore

by **John Ford**

In order of speaking:

Bonaventura, *a friar*	**Richard Cordery**
Giovanni, *son to Florio*	**Rupert Graves**
Vasques, *servant to Soranzo*	**Clive Francis**
Grimaldi, *a Roman gentleman*	**Paul Stewart**
Florio, *a citizen of Parma*	**Ron Pember**
Donado, *another citizen*	**Roger Hammond**
Soranzo, *a nobleman*	**Michael Simkins**
Putana, *tutress to Annabella*	**Bridget Turner**
Annabella, *daughter to Florio*	**Suzan Sylvester**
Bergetto, *nephew to Donado*	**Russell Dixon**
Poggio, *servant to Bergetto*	**Jim Barclay**
Richardetto, *a supposed physician*	**Struan Rodger**
Philotis, *his niece*	**Georgie Glen**
Hippolita, *wife to Richardetto*	**Polly Adams**
Officer	**Peter Dineen**
Servant to the Cardinal	**Adrian Jubb**
A Cardinal, *nuncio to the Pope*	**Nigel Bellairs**

Banditti, Officers, Servants, Guests, Dancers
Carol Been, David Crossley, Brenda Dowsett, Kate Dyson, Michelle Evans, Jennifer Hill, Captain Keane'o', Ian McLaren, Rosemary O'Boyle, Anthony Sergeant, Frank Stirling, Alan Towner, Alan White

Musicians: **Paul Todd** (*Music director/keyboards*), **Michael Brain** (*wind instruments*), **Steven Craven** (*trumpet*), **Howard Evans** (*trumpet*), **Robin Jeffrey** (*lute*), **Andrew Robinson** (*wind instruments*), **Anthony Wagstaff** (*percussion*)

Director	**Alan Ayckbourn**
Settings	**Roger Glossop**
Costumes	**Sally Gardner**
Lighting	**Mick Hughes**
Music	**Paul Todd**
Fights arranged by	**Malcolm Ranson**
Dances arranged by	**David Toguri**
Staff Director **Kenneth Mackintosh**	Production Manager **Andrew Peat**
Stage Manager **Courtney Bryant**	Deputy Stage Manager **Lesley Walmsley**
Assistant Stage Managers **Marc W Dugmore, Brewyeen Rowland**	Sound **Richard Borkum**
Assistant to Roger Glossop **Paul Farnsworth**	Assistant to the Lighting Designer **Tim Bray**
Assistant Production Manager **George Ellerington**	Costume Supervisor **Stephanie Baird**

The Scene: **Parma**

Opening: **The Olivier Theatre 3 March 1988**

Length: about 2½ hours including 20-minute interval

The actors in this production are the NT group working under the direction of Alan Ayckbourn. They are also in A *Small Family Business* in the Olivier

Programme written and compiled by **Tim Goodwin**; designed by **Michael Mayhew** and **Rose Towler**; cover (and poster) designed by **Richard Bird**

Production photographed by **Nobby Clark**

runs for. And don't forget to list the Director, Producer, stage crew – everyone concerned with the production of the play, including yourself as Press and Marketing Manager.

You should also include prominent information about refreshments. What is available? Where?

Once your audience have found out about the practical details of their evening, they will want to enjoy reading about the play itself: you could feature the actor who plays Billy in a discussion with the director. Was it easy to portray Billy's character? Which aspects of Billy's role did he find difficult? Perhaps Mrs Casper could feature as well. Did the actor playing Billy's mother find it possible to sympathise with her difficulties? You could even find poems that illuminate some of the themes in **Kes** to interest your audience further. Start with the Vernon Scannell poem on page 29 if you like.

For added interest present a number of advertisements for firms and businesses who are giving sponsorship to the theatre. Include an advertisement for future productions at the theatre!

For those of you who are computer buffs, why not make use of a word processor for these assignments? That, combined with computer graphics and the design talents of your class, should produce some impressive results.

Acknowledgements

The authors and publishers would like to thank the following for their kind permission to reproduce copyright texts in this volume:
Lemon and Durbridge Ltd for quotations from *Kes* by Barry Hines and Allan Stronach. All rights in this play are strictly reserved. Any enquiries concerning amateur and professional performing rights should be made before rehearsal to: Lemon and Durbridge Limited, 24 Pottery Lane, Holland Park, London W11 4LZ. No performance may be made unless a licence has been obtained. Michael Joseph Ltd for extracts from *A Kestrel for a Knave* by Barry Hines; Associated Book Publishers (UK) Ltd for the extract from *The Secret Diary of Adrian Mole Aged 13¾* by Sue Townsend published by Methuen London; The Hogarth Press for the extract from *Cider with Rosie* by Laurie Lee; A. M. Heath, Sonia Brownell Orwell and Martin Secker & Warburg for 'The Road to Wigan Pier' by George Orwell; Laurence Pollinger Ltd and the Estate of Mrs Frieda Lawrence Ravagli for 'Last Lesson of the Afternoon' by D. H. Lawrence; Robson Books Ltd for 'Incendiary' by Vernon Scannell published in *New and Collected Poems 1950–1980*.

The authors and publishers would also like to thank the following for permission to use illustrations and photographs: Kent County Libraries for the library interior on page 3; Barnaby's Picture Library for the photograph by Peter O'Reilly on page 8, and the photographs on page 35; The National Film Archive for the photographs on pages 11, 17, 24, 29; Piccadilly Radio for the photograph on page 12; The Kobal Collection for the photograph on page 15; Bob Irwin for the photograph on page 31 (bottom); Popperfoto for the photograph on page 45; The National Theatre for the illustrations on pages 46 and 47. Information on the copyright holders for photographs on pages 7, 14 and 31 (top) would be gratefully received.